Favorite Pets

I can draw!

Favorite Pets

Learn to draw furry friends
and cute companions step by step!

This library edition published in 2015 by Walter Foster Jr.,
an imprint of Quarto Publishing Group USA Inc.
6 Orchard Road, Suite 100
Lake Forest, CA 92630

Distributed in the United States and Canada by
Lerner Publisher Services
241 First Avenue North
Minneapolis, MN 55401 U.S.A.
www.lernerbooks.com

First Library Edition

Library of Congress Cataloging-in-Publication Data

Legendre, Philippe.
  Favorite pets / by Philippe Legendre. -- First Library Edition.
    pages cm
  ISBN 978-1-939581-55-6
1. Animals in art--Juvenile literature. 2. Drawing--Technique--Juvenile literature. I. Legendre, Philippe, illustrator.
II. Title.
  NC783.8.P48O85 2015
  743.6--dc23

                                                                    2014026657

9 8 7 6 5 4 3 2

Table of Contents

Tools & Materials

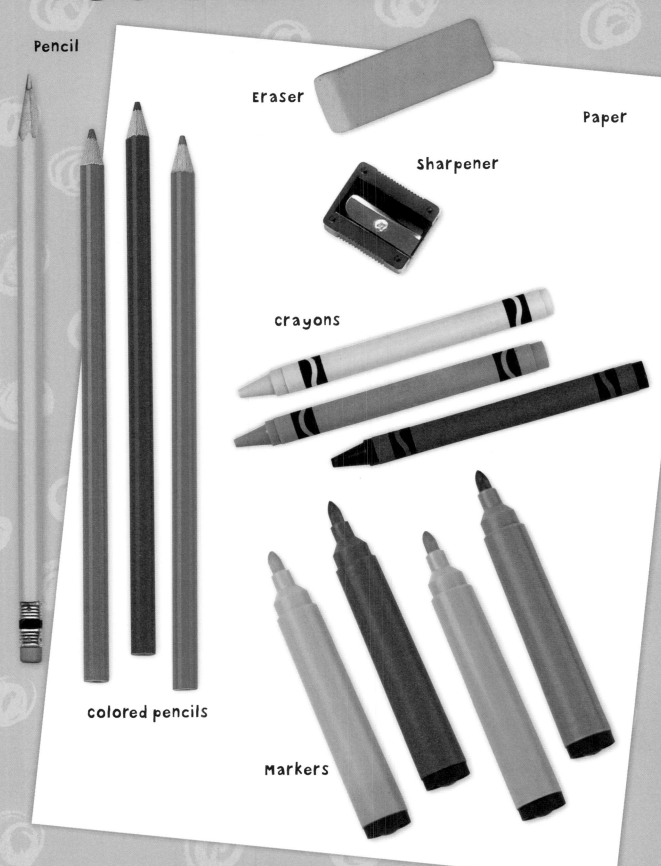

Pencil

Eraser

Paper

Sharpener

crayons

colored pencils

Markers

The Color Wheel

The color wheel shows the relationships between colors. It helps us understand how the different colors relate to and react with one another. It's easy to make your own color wheel!

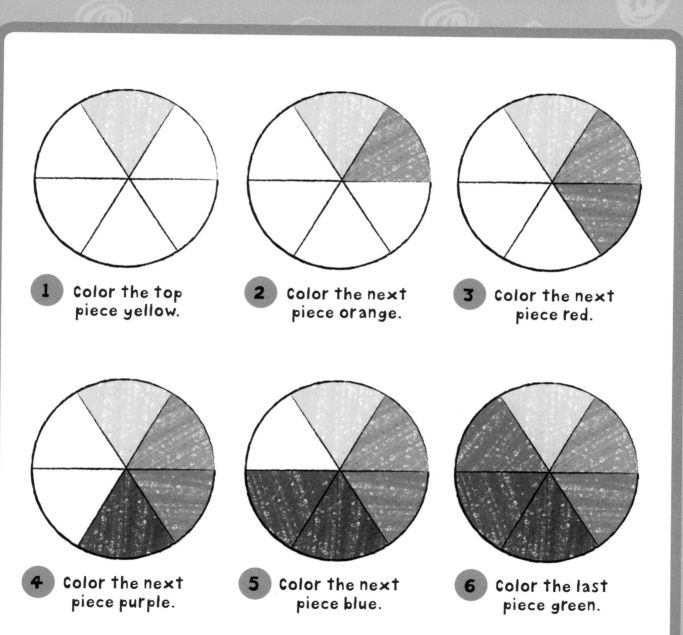

1. Color the top piece yellow.

2. Color the next piece orange.

3. Color the next piece red.

4. Color the next piece purple.

5. Color the next piece blue.

6. Color the last piece green.

Getting Started

Warm up your hand by drawing some squiggles and shapes on a piece of scrap paper.

Draw a square

Draw an oval

Draw a circle

Draw a rectangle

Draw a triangle

If you can draw a few basic shapes, you can draw just about anything!

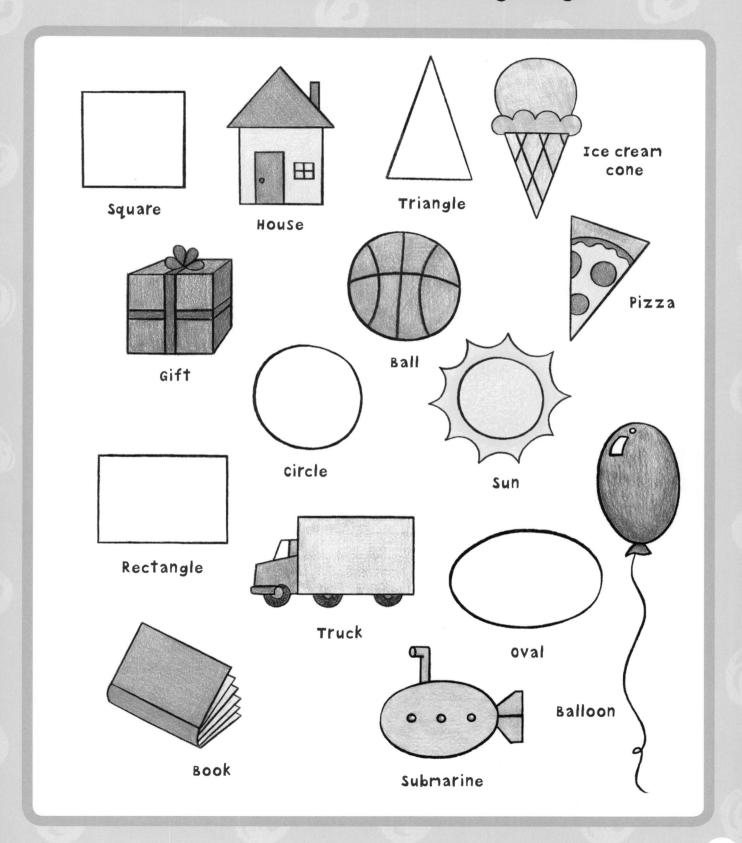

Square

House

Triangle

Ice cream cone

Gift

Ball

Pizza

circle

Sun

Rectangle

Truck

Oval

Balloon

Book

Submarine

orange Tabby

This kitty is gentle and playful, and it loves sunbathing!

11

Husky

Huskies are athletic sled dogs with thick coats and beautiful eyes.

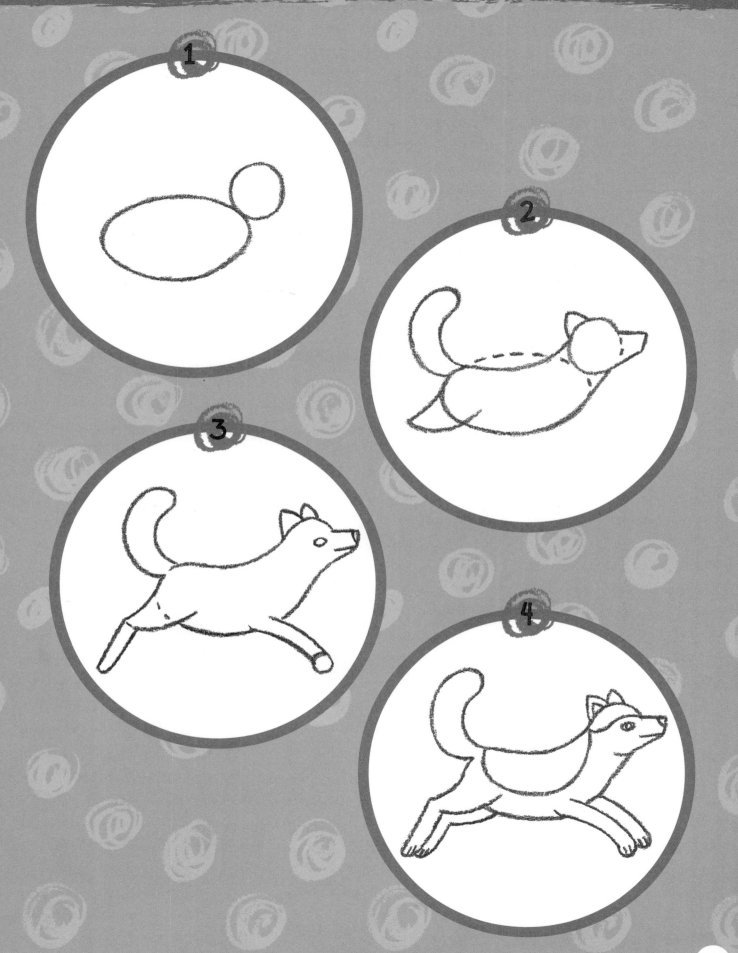

Goldfish

This pet comes in a variety of colors, including red, black, white, yellow, orange, and gold.

15

Pony

A pony is a small horse that is gentle and docile in nature.

17

Black cat

This cat likes to explore his neighborhood at night!

Labrador Retriever

This gentle dog likes to play outside with her pup!

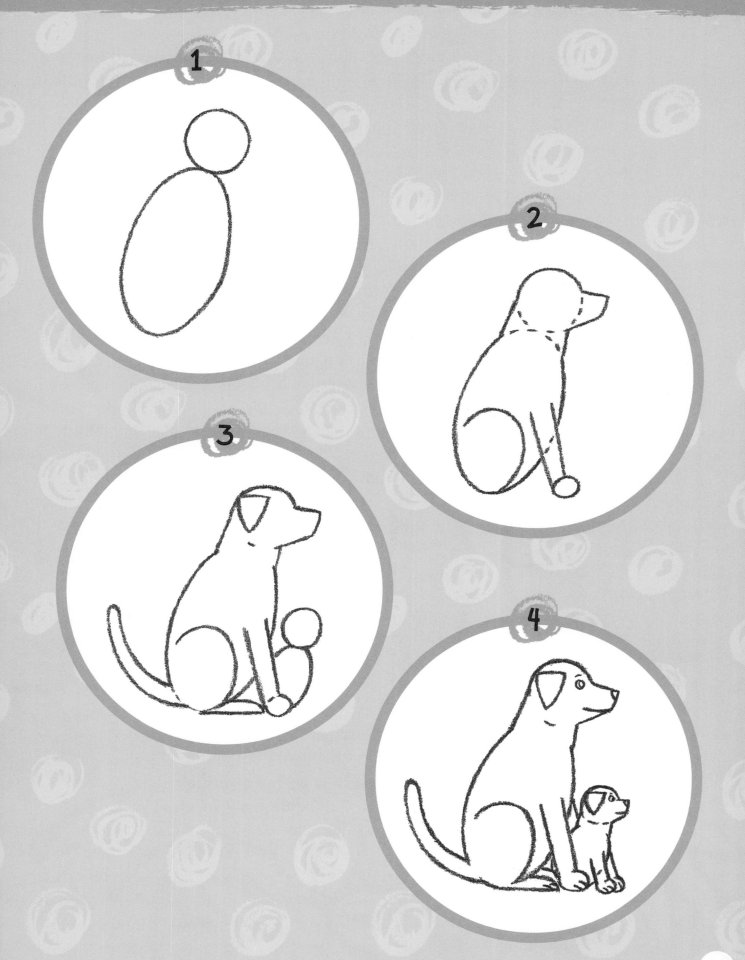

Rabbit

This cute little bunny likes to hop around in the garden!

Horse & Colt

This mommy horse loves to run around with her colt!

1

2

3

4

Napping cat

Napping is a kitty's favorite hobby, aside from playing of course!

Jack Russell Terrier

This small dog is full of energy and likes to run around and hunt!

Turtle

This reptile swims in freshwater and explores on land!

Foal

Draw this young horse playing in a field.

Fox Terrier

This energetic terrier likes to play outside!

Mouse

This squeaky pet likes to run around and play at night!

Mustang

This wild horse likes to run through the grass!

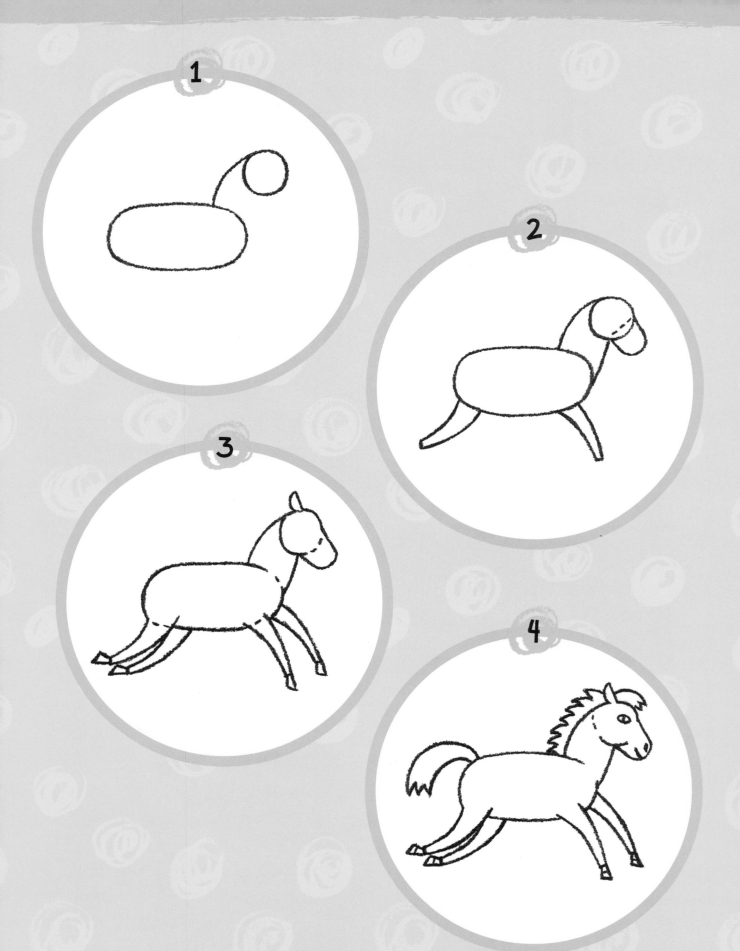

Persian cat

This long-haired cat is affectionate and friendly!

Dalmatian Puppies

These friendly pups are ready to play!

Guinea Pig

This cute, friendly pet loves attention!

Parakeet

This parrot has brightly colored green and yellow feathers.

The End